CONFLICTED LIGHT

J.P. DANCING BEAR

salmonpoetry

Published in 2008 by
Salmon Poetry,
Cliffs of Moher, County Clare, Ireland
Website: www.salmonpoetry.com
email: info@salmonpoetry.com

Copyright © J.P. Dancing Bear, 2008

ISBN 978-1-903392-73-7

All Rights Reserved. No part of this publication may be reproduced or transmitted in any form or by any means, electronic or mechanical, including photocopy, recording, or any information storage or retrieval system, without permission in writing from the publisher. The book is sold subject to the condition that it shall not, by way of trade or otherwise, be lent, resold or otherwise circulated without the publisher's prior consent in any form of binding or cover other than that in which it is published and without a similar condition, including this condition being imposed on the subsequent purchaser.

Cover artwork "Beat of Wings" by Franziska Turek
http://franziskaturek.exto.nl/

for Rain

Table of Contents

Conflicts

Natural Enemies	11
Election Season	12
Jesus in America	13
Cain in America	14
After the Dawn of the Patriot Act	16
The Garden of War	17
Salvation Nation	19
March	20
Casida of the Mojave	21
The Practice Horn	22
Casida of Ryan Seacrest's Shiny New Coat	23
Diorama	24
My Yehiro	25

Exit Strategies

Last Christmas	28
Canaries	29
Oral History	30
The Patient	31
Last Hour	32
Chorale	33
Elegy to the Living	34
After the Diagnosis	35
Departing Phoenix	36
Accidental	37
Eurydice Lost	38
Orpheus the Thief	39
Extra Innings	40
Elysian Fields	41

Armistice Days

The Arrogance of Finite Fauna	45
Without End	46
When We Are Stewards	47

The February Horses	48
Storm Watch with Cows	49
Auricle	50
Wintering	51
Seen Through a Vase of Flowers	52
The Weather, Like a Pop Song Stuck in the Mind	53
Long Shadows at Play in the Field	54
Coyote Star	55
Wasp Hour	56
Here, the Lily	57
Believing in Fire	58
The Dandelion as the Wise One on the Mountain	59

AFTERMATHS

You and Not You Drawing a Bath	63
Paper Soul	64
The Lost Lyre	65
The Hidden Cells	66
Sirens	67
Medusa in Smallville	68
Circe Waiting	69
Dreaming Poetry of Hydrogen	70
Woman and Window Light	71
Casida of a Rising Woman	72
The Cannonball	73
More Than Sound	76
Ulysses Takes the A-Train to Calypso's Apartment	77
Persephone at the Farmers' Market	78
Your Star Chart is Finite	79
Against Against Metaphor	80
Snow Globe Life	81
Idol	82
After Reading Your Letters	83
Sonnet	84
Birthday Note	86

*When you take up your palette, a bullet hole in its wing,
you call on the light that brings the olive tree to life.*
—Federico Garcia Lorca,
"Ode to Salvador Dali"

1. Conflicts

Natural Enemies

all day the owl is dreaming of a crow, dreaming
of a crow, dreaming of a crow and his war caw
rushing through the pines, and the owl opens
her mouth as if to say wait, wait until nightfall,
until nightfall when the crow's own blackness
is not enough to hide him from her keen eyes.

all night the crow is dreaming of an owl, dreaming
of an owl, dreaming of an owl and battle screech
so close it could run through his dark body and sever
his spine. his mouth moves in silence: wait, wait
until daybreak when the owl's gray camouflage
cannot protect her from the murders of crows.

in twilight the owl and crow are praying to live, praying
to live, praying to live the long hours of hunting. they do
not fly nor tempt the other into the unowned time
and orange territory of conflicted light. they bide, bide
in their pine churches with their psalms to a god
who would favor their feathers over the other's.

ELECTION SEASON

The old politicians are on their way
to the tall ashes of the state, beyond all hope
of green and lighted fields before the hills.

In a different place, the dead might drift
down the river as campaigners move
into the weeds of the pale city, set up camps,
alive with promises of work. But it is Autumn
and the geese have already begun to feel
the fading light within their wings.

The volunteers can hardly feel the cold
as they pin another button on the coat
of a slender farm child. The gray light does
not fill these skies with hope;
neither can the pumpkins manifesting
themselves in the twilight;
nor the ghosts of river boats
paddling slowly against the current.

The candidates flow into the city with the moon
upon the withering fields white with frost.
All are reflecting a brightness
that is not theirs to keep or give.

JESUS IN AMERICA

He stands on the corner
of Market Street
with hands agape at his sides.
Each tear from his eye reflects
the city's starvation.
He opens his doors, the robes
of his church,
to reveal the neon heart
blinking through its thorns;
he looks up the huge golden arcs
of fast food reaching for heaven
from across the street.
He is the bun of God,
the cola of deliverance.

CAIN COMES TO AMERICA

Innocence has gone
missing from the fields.

Cain, God created
the devil in your heart—

not for you to excuse
murder, but to believe

in God's capacity.
Whisper what you will

into the flight recorder.
Fire is not the only way

God speaks.
The workers of the fields

have stopped—
gone to plow the rubble.

Blood has begun to rise,
humming like an angel

over the red heart of America.
Through the growling voice

of twisted girders,
shattered glass,

God asks you
Where is your brother?!

After the Dawn of the Patriot Act

All during the sun's olympic willful triumphant arc
I watched banners and flags rise. I thought a parade
had commenced down Main Street, but the music was
a hiving hum and a rumble of tanks. A low chant
of revenge hung in the air like bats blackening at dusk
ready to cover the moon. The people closest to me
had been replicated, replaced by mannequins with echo
chambers in their chests. They became megaphone-
mouthpieces of marching orders, and of distrust—they
were the new never-blink neighbor in the window,
suspicious and on the phone to police about everything
they thought was out of place in my yard. Our days
were filled with small chatter of *American Idol*
and *Desperate Housewives*. At night I lit a thin candle
in remembrance; in quiet light I wrote letters to missing
friends gone on to a place where nothing is read or saved.

The Garden of War

I can only think salt when news comes
that the snails are mounting an offensive—
"An assault on green" My Press Secretary
calls it even though this is selective truth.

My Secretary of Defense refuses to use
the word poison, but it is his recommendation
that the weapons are deployed.
My cabinet assures me we are right

and should stay the course; they talk
of *collateral damage* and *acceptable risk*.
I order the carpet bombing with pellets.
At the dinner hour, I address the country

with they are not like us. Even though
we hunger the same. I root out
the snail food and plant my vision
of their homeland. I do what's best

for the region. I ignore my protestors
and opponents — they're all traitors
anyway. I can only think of salt.
All the time salt like a dried up ocean,

a great flat of death, stealing moisture
from the soil. If my support slips,
I will order a launch and scorch the earth—
who will say I'm weak? Let my enemies

gather in candlelight vigils. Let them weep
and wail. Let them cry *mistake, mistake*.
I will never admit it, there will be no recourse,
and in time we will all forget.

SALVATION NATION

He is the messiah of all you survey;
out of the barn door, the messiah is saving
trees and the small frogs who live there.

He is in love with everyone, though no one
shows him a return—bad prophet margin.
But he keeps his feet steeped in the dust

of desert walking. He is a university
of applied ignorance, Cheek-turner. Someone
is pulling the doors of his robe open, gasping

at the scars and wounds of his walls.
Today's lesson is economy, *the weight of a dove
in silver, if you can tell the class the true cost*

of ignoring love. —He is the messiah of riddlers,
teaching us to fish out the answers
hidden in the deep mirror of ourselves.

He is the king of the small fisted hearts
knotted in wishes for decent treatment;
he is the doctor on the threshold

our mothers once told us about. We hear
the knocking and our doors fling open
hoping he will fix us free of charge
never knowing he is here and needs saving.

MARCH

Suddenly this hunger,
this war.
Everything is going gray.
All greens, all browns
turning gray.
And the burning,
a ghostly amber light
through ash.
Yet the streets appear
cold with winter snow.
From curb to curb, no car
or foot — the avenue
vacant makes me think
of plowed fields waiting
for the tillers;
waiting for farmers
to rise from their trenches,
their foxholes and return,
return
to Spring,
to their lives among broad
leaves.

CASIDA OF THE MOJAVE

To see you naked is to know the Earth.
—Federico Garcia Lorca

And all night the desert dreams of horses
rippling their muscles through a tall grass
far from stretches of sand and tumbleweed.

Does the desert dream of another like a lover,
a missing piece, a split-apart; or would it desire
the caress of ocean or meadow against its body?

Within the desert's heart stirs a rattlesnake of envy
and a cornered scorpion. What tenderness can be
extended is offered in the darting body of a jack rabbit.

And what have you brought to the desert's nakedness:
angering garbage strewn along blacktop strips, she
swallows your atomic tests like blood from a cut lip.

The desert screams *Lover, No! Lover, no lover*, over
again, but it is like horse hooves in sand, roots
of tumbleweed, the leftover glass of a bomb blast.

The Practice Horn

Because his lips must never rest
upon the burning rim
of the mouthpiece. He still needs
to rehearse the pushing
air from his lungs
into the near sound
   of everything coming down.
It is the almost music of the final
   message. The eleventh hours spent
crumbling small stones—
pretending they are cities.

He will get it right
again and again, with metronome
   persistence; he stays
up late in his room
cheeks ballooned and pressing
the note that will doom his listeners.

Casida of Ryan Seacrest's Shiny New Coat

Because there must be a mic stand for every young Orpheus.
   The demigod judges are looking for a foil.

A much needed sacrifice of wink-smiling
to the giant red cola can in the sky.

The audience is in need of pandering and glad
hands. All the while on our little man-made island

(not unlike the kidney shaped isle of 3
hour tours), we are trained callers in the bank

of telephone polls, worried about our favorite
image of young americans, while the metronome

of automatic gunfire, timpani car bombs and a chorus
of burning rubble is the common soundtrack

sublime, rolling at the edges of our subconscious
commercial breaks—*news at 11*—when we're all ready

   asleep.

Diorama

The girl in the gymnasium waves,
points into the box: A farm
with an old man on a John Deere
plowing the fields, a barn with hay
and horses to eat it, some cows,
a chicken coop and pig pen. Rows
of corn spreading to the artificial
horizon of the cardboard back wall.
Inside the house with its roostered
weathervane, a mother stands
at the kitchen window, washing
vegetables in the sink, preparing
dinner and humming a harvest song.
She's anxiously eyeing a vehicle, black
as a tornado, pulling into the drive.

My Yeriho

1.
A familiar silhouette draws me inward and across
the desert. Not a Pilgrimage. Nor Command.
A shadow of a temple on the dunes.

The fortifications and ramparts erected
with a long battle in mind. Each brick coerced
into a place; each subject ordered to stand—

indentured servitude and demand.
Like all cities are built. Cradled civilization.
City of my father-where stones are raised

to look like men. If there are tears in the desert—
the thirsty have drink. Each of us holds
a Dead Sea behind our eyes.

2.
People who look like me live behind the walls—
obeying the whipcrack, bending to hunger,
gambling their crumbs.

Locked doors, dead bolt comfort against
agents of the unknown. The curfew comes
earlier each night. The stone golems

patrolling. People who look like me
are saying *yes* and showing their documents
of citizenship. They don't see

how many sons make a foundation
from their bodies, or how many others
betray their training and give bread
and board to strangers.

3.
The trumpets of my army unit.
Is this how jazz is born? With the dust
of a place like this coating your fingers.

Could suffering be held within a single note?
The first master musician would love
and release such music to the air.

I hated this city even before I pressed my ear
to the gate. I heard the false god praised.
Each sacrifice was called out

like a religion. I readied my horn and filled
my lungs with terrible, divine air,
I ballooned my cheeks to the mouthpiece
and pressed down on the piston.

2. Exit Strategies

LAST CHRISTMAS

Her face was the rim in a crater
of the moon. I could see the sharp
bones jutting through her skin—
river stones in silt.

Something in my chest fell in—
crashing in the dark. My father
lifted her skeleton from the chair.
Their shadows broke on chipped

paint walls. Someone muttered
morphine as though it was another
name for Death. I was a journeyman
village idiot, aspiring to court jester.

A family of half smiles and denial.
Our children played outside—a form
of disbelief. They kept saying:
Next year... Someday... All of us...

Canaries

My grandmother's hands are canaries
ready to collapse in on themselves.
I study her hand in mine:
the thin skin, the purple veins and bones

ready to collapse in on themselves.
I am crying an afternoon of
the thin skin, the purple veins and bones
behind my attempts to be brave.

I am crying an afternoon of
my grandmother trying to communicate
behind my attempts to be brave.
I feel her hand slipping—

my grandmother trying to communicate
after the stroke stole her voice.
I feel her hand slipping
to make the gestures lost in air

after the stroke stole her voice,
locked inside her head, left
to make gestures that are lost in air
Between us,

locked inside, her head left,
ready to collapse in on itself.
Between us,
my grandmother's hands are canaries.

Oral History

Photographs
of relatives and their friends;
forgotten names
my grandmother used to tell me.
Monochrome shadows—
a family history.
Their faces do not hold
the same meaning for me
they did for her.
I have no memories
of them, fond or otherwise.
Most died before I was born.
I keep them,
I am not certain
why,
but on summer days
when the black widows crawl inside,
I pull the shadows from storage
and strain to hear my her voice—
a stroke in history
explaining who was who.

The Patient

His tray is a still-life of an over-ripe banana,
vanilla pudding and a splash spring flowers
from the younger patient's bed next to his.

He stews at how his neighbor ignores visitors,
the bounty of get-well cards and bright bouquets.
He would hold and cherish the green stems

as if they had blossomed an extra year of life.

Last Hour

When, after many sutures, the scalpel
edges to set loose of you,

       it relinquishes your fragile shell
in the milk carton white

       of a hospital room, leaves you a testament
of bandages and stitches

with winter's obnoxious raging at the window.

Tonight there is a vision

hovering above your head: a halo, spinning,
golden and humming

with the harp of your ribs.

And is that the winged voice of your mother,
       not weeping but washing your wounds?

She says, *Oh child, follow me*,
       into this last first snow.

Chorale

There is a music that only the dead can hear
with their perfected voices, clean tones,
like a child's wet finger ringing a glass—
and this is what Orpheus brought back,
what he did not let go.

My father did not play an instrument,
no summoning trumpet, no dream of Satchmo.
His voice might be a single note held, in the mouth
of a tenor saxophone—bright, resplendent
and widening like the Mississippi.
He reverberates the branches of the aspens
and breathes over their roots. And then silence
and another soul delivers his note.

This is not midnight music, not the witching hour's,
not heard while in the fog-hugged graveyards.
The tones are twilit, something caught
while one leg is on the ground and the other in bed.
The space between diurnal and nocturnal creatures
where a song does not haunt but opens to breath.
That single moment when you can nearly recall
where your fingers went as a child practicing piano.

ELEGY TO THE LIVING

I want no more sutures in my life, no obnoxious
stitches in my carton, the anxious testament
of the body's failure. No dreams of stature
for me either. No dignity in another round
of tests or what they've meant, no more cretin
orderlies. Just the certainty of an oblong
box: so sure of its mature wood. No knocks
against bad luck. And spare me the smattering
of charming chatter on my behalf—make yourself
feel better, if that's what you need, but leave
my interests out of it. Save the weeping—
it adds to my uncontrollable guilt, not being
there to comfort the ones I love. Give me
no inlaid art, decorative for the living eye
but of no use for the other side. Toss me
a flower, white as a sheet, upon the water. Say
farewell, say so long, say good-bye. Watch me
become smaller as the current ripples away.

AFTER THE DIAGNOSIS

This is the body's Dark Age, the long period of forgetfulness.
I am a feudal king issuing laws about witchcraft and taxes.
Armies are raised to war with the neighboring kingdoms,
there is blood from the battles in the barley fields and orchards.
Only the Church keeps the written word alive with its monks
scribbling into the dank nights of candle smoke and silence.
My knights swear fealty over a handwritten bible, promising
their souls to God and my sovereign declarations and claims.
In these times, it is easy to fall into the belief of dragons,
the sleeping princesses and winking old vagabond soothsayers;
so easy to see fairy circles, phookas, and ghost kings at midnight.
The astrologers point their sextants at strange alignments
in the cosmos and conjecture that one myth conjoined
with another means there will be a great flood — a washing
of the land. My Shakespeare, my Da Vinci are waiting
in their fetal positions, waiting for my Charlemagne
to gather an administration. There are whispers of Jesus
returning with judgement; fear of apocalypse spreads
wings over the world. This is not a time for reason
or science, but perseverance and prayer — tilling the soil
and kissing the rosary beads. I am waiting for a sign,
waiting for new light to break through the stained glass sky.

Departing Phoenix

I swallow bird songs that do not resurface—
if I opened my wrists, they will fly out.

I fall into necessity again,
at a gas station, unable to pay

for the fuel, yet yearning for the road.
The attendant balances a pencil

on her nose and talks of the circus returning.
I am flashbulbs of flirtation and shame;

whichever currency is required.
Her register drawer shuts but stays hungry.

A big-lettered sign says not to smoke,
but everywhere there is talk of matches.

In the empurpled desert light
I am an old Buick speeding over a cliff:

seconds of brilliant air singing past my face,
before impact, ignition, my unfurling black

and orange tongue. Oh let me be a song,
a wing of ash escaping from the wreckage.

Accidental

With rain, the streets
trickle their black-
top music to the sky.
What was blue
has joined with gray,
and the green light
changes to yellow
then scattered
pieces of scarlet.
Her hair is wet asphalt.
From any window
I hear her whisper
among the coats
and umbrellas, unseen—
a ghost taken
for granted.
The small faces
that are not hers
drift by like wrappers
and autumn leaves.

Tomorrow broken snow
will lie like a body
waiting for mourners.

EURYDICE LOST

On the boulevard she hears a clarion tone
reach into the underworld below her skin, whirl-
wind her senses, morals, a thing not unlike love.

She rolls down the window and slows her car.
Searching for the source, she cannot focus on all
of the tail lights, the wheels, the colored bodies.

He leaves this world one more pure anonymous note.

ORPHEUS THE THIEF

The angry Dead can still hear music, slight of hand,
all his emotions deftly plucked in heart-struck tones.
They won't be moved again by any sound so grand.

The Underworld decreed all music had been banned—
though the tune still hums in their heads; in their bones
the angry Dead can still sense music, slight of hand.

That con man nimbly played a lyric to command
the hasty release of his love, now one they owned—
they won't be moved again by any sound so grand.

O how they wanted to believe this clever man
who waded through the blacker waters all alone
to play the Dead his sad music. By slight of hand,

he swore his fervid love for her (they'd understand).
How could they deny the only love he'd ever known?
Surely they'd be moved by such a sentiment so grand.

The Underworld gave in to his ardent demand
and were made fools of-he dropped her like a stone.
The angry dead can still hear music. Slight of Hand,
they won't be moved again by any sound so grand.

EXTRA INNINGS

An errand wind circled the bases.
In the dusk, the outfielders purpled.
Their bodies bent as if braced to hold
the expanding night on their backs.
Humming, the park lights stood
like strange sentinels.

In the dug-outs, the men mouthed
words close to a prayer.
Still more quietly they made wishes
to never stop the play. Their faces
aged in darkening twilight.

I was a shadow in the stands
filled with the tension of extra innings.
Fans pulled on their team jackets
and backed further into their seats.
Halos of gnats swarm above our heads.

With two outs and a full count,
I whispered my own dark wish:
a game that might be the longest
something for record books,
something to say, "I had been there when…"
But the batter connected with a crack,
and the stitched ghost of my hopes rose
out of the park, swallowed by the night air.

ELYSIAN FIELDS

In the salmon and tin light of dawn I'm still
in last night's dream, arms stiff in my red wing
blackbird shirt. Green sheets — was I possessed
to have bought them? They hill and glen over
the landscape of my bed wanting flowers, cypress,
aspen, linden, and pine; wanting what is left
of the winter to trickle and stream. And why
have I risen like Orpheus — And looked back
upon these fields of peace? I dress like a cadaver:
a suit and black tie to match the half-circles
of my eyes. Sleep vagues my mind. I walk past
the gates of the other undead, past the asphodel red
with the want of bees, past the pleas of hundreds
of Euridyces asking, *Why, why would you ever leave?*

3. Armistice Days

THE ARROGANCE OF FINITE FAUNA

He believed himself a better flower
than the rest. *Hush*, he'd think,
*A rush of wind sets through my petals
like song.* Pray to the perfection
of being alone. He knew what it was
to attract the bees he could never please,
sending them frustrated away
to look for his equal when there
was none. No one could match his
nine-petal face or his slender stem.

He would argue with a hungry fawn:
if devoured, there could never be
another to replace his broad green
blades, outstretched toward the water.
He went on gazing, long after the sun
had sunk, after the skunks
and the coyotes crept out to scrounge
the refuse of the day. He was one
flower refusing to close, denying
the late hour so he could pose
and show up a field of constellations.
He said, to the audience in his head,
*Even the stars fall at the sight of me—
and who could blame those dull flames?*
But he could not see the larger world
Had brightly learned to ignore such a bore.

WITHOUT END

In those out-of-school mornings
when we'd wander the dry weeds
and the locusts, searching for the dead,
we'd find their shriveled eyes,
their splayed wings, and lines of ants
making away with the meat.
We'd dig the graves with spoons,
roll the bodies in—afraid to touch them
and catch the lice our mothers
always warned us would be waiting.

David Buehler was our priest—
he went to church every Sunday.
He'd stand at the head
of the patted-down mounds
with their popsicle stick crosses;
we'd bow our heads and he'd recite
a prayer: *O God, whose days are without end...*
Even the locusts quieted.

At noon,
when our shadows were tight beneath us,
we'd watch the souls rise,
watery and wavering, from the fields.
We'd dream we'd done good deeds,
that our souls would follow some day.

When We Are Stewards

We will each pick a wild species
we pledge our lives to,
learn their movements
and moods, take their name
into our name, keep their calls
within our voices. In winter,
some of us will hibernate,
others will follow migratory paths,
or unearth stashes of food
we'd spent the other seasons saving:
This is my gift of acorns—
may it last like a grove of oaks.
This is my marsh summer home
I share with you. Welcome
to my den, let our bodies slow
to love. Here is my ancestral
burial ground-may we return
as our animal wards.

THE FEBRUARY HORSES
—*after a painting by Grant Wood*

What can I say to them? Charcoal smudges
against snow. Their barbed-wire stares cut
into my skin—cold, the color of rust,

old blood. Their shadows are arching hills,
hoofprint valleys, everything that is
windswept and worn. Three wise faces

waiting for me to slip the loop that holds
two sections of fence together.
There are no arguments, no pleas—they know

before I do that I am here only to release
their bodies into the world, to leap
into the black chasm that separates us.

Storm Watch with Cows

There are cows in a field of black rain.
The skeletons of trees opposed by lightning.
There is a hint of mist rising from the ground.
And I wonder who cares for these creatures.

Where is the skinny lad who tends them?
Is he waving his way through the scruffy
ears of corn, dull green and gold, stopping
to think of a girl who lived a mile away.

She was the apple of the summer swimming hole,
eyes dark as a cow's, deep as evening ravines.
She is gone the way dust is swept from a porch,
the foreclosure notice pinned to the front door.

Perhaps it is the way this landscape gathers
and presents itself like a scene from *Hamlet*
with its graveyard of worn skulls and the memory
of a girl drowning just off stage in a downpour.

Her hair swaying in the same rhythm as corn
waiting for a combine. He sees them out there,
those ghostly cows, as more of loss, something
that belongs to horizons, a respectful distance.

He knows the time of year, the clacking season
of cattle cars nears. So maybe he's slow to tend
the herd, hoping to give them a little more
freedom, a little more time life before the storm.

AURICLE

I heard the humming engine
of a heart smaller than an anvil;
in the hummingbird's forest
my ear was mistaken for a flower—
I should be complimented
for the brief moment before
the taste of my ear canal
will forever mark the thin tongue.
The hunger that was whispered
to me, woke me from a dream:

I was the drum in the redwoods,
the tongue of green prophecies,
the anvil of summer hunger,
awakened to the canopy songs
that had lain in the linens of leaves
I called my stomach. Now I hear
the hammer's rumor of sparks
on the anvil and can taste fear.
Now I realize I worked for years
in the coded silence of a paper heart.

WINTERING

Now Winter's light splashes into the open pond—
green and brown feathers, webbed feet.
I've been waiting since they left last Spring.

I recognize them by names no one ever uttered,
but I assigned to them. They talk that nasal language
and everything is a flutter and a flailing.

And where is the Summer right now? Where
did it fly? I cannot see any sign of Canada
upon them. They do not preen Idaho from their plumes.

It is so silly gaining comfort from their return,
as if God stares out of their eyes and squawks
everything works, everything always works.

Seen Through a Vase of Flowers
—*after a painting by George Ault*

These yellow eyes, rimmed in red, unwitnessing
me in my cut-stem life. Already a petal fallen
from a place where the pupil naturally goes.

The daffodils are fading, drooping, yellow tongues
thirsty, and puckered, their gray lips—
not looking at each other, as if lost in argument.

The green has dulled among these white skulls—
twisted and bent as though waiting for a wind
to help them wave as arms might—*so long*.

I am drawn to the large irises staring me down,
naked and disquietingly round, I remember
my love, she stood like this and I fell like a leaf.

THE WEATHER, LIKE A POP SONG STUCK IN THE MIND

He began to see the morning wind,
swirls of fog formed words in a language
he had never spoken. A skin of clouds

and geese formed on the lake. A galaxy
of gnats rose above the reeds. Blossoms
pushed their white fragrance through the mist.
He hummed a song stuck in his mind,

the one of which he only knew one line,
over and over—pressing against his throat.
He thought of warblers, and if they too
had a few words or a bar trapped
in their beaks. What if the next chorus
could have broken the morning
into a bright blue dome and a blaring sun?

Long Shadows at Play in the Field

Forgive the cornfields and harvests
and their slip song of autumn
pushing against earth's own shadow;

Spring's leftover fanfare is on the ground
in yellowed, flecking red, cell walls
breaking, breaking back into soil—

and this is the scent of death:
ripe fruit, the first dew caught in frost.
I have been pulled down

into the world of music—combines,
tillers, hoes, the beginning movement
of an operatic wind tugging,

tugging my shirt, as though I were
a leaf, loose in the air and ready
to be turned and returned to the dirt.

Forgive desire closing its eye,
the long sleep of wanting to learn
a new thing or exact some change

in the way this land is lined into rows,
waiting, open for seeds, furrows—against
the promise of cold on the ground.

Coyote Star

A star steps on the shoulder of a mountain,
its fire rests in a pillow of redwoods, bright,
a beacon demanding an entourage of wise men.

Who am I to be here, out of place, hypnotized
by its luminous trek?   I am gilded with shadow,
so rooted I can feel leaves tremble.

I am caught in the whiteness of the star's body,
raising its wings to fly across night's indigo sea.
I know how long its light has taken to reach me.

I hear the coyotes crooning a melancholy tune
about a beckoning love and the distance.
I keep my ear in my hand, listening as they fade.

WASP HOUR

As a golden needle threads the air
I consider the thinness of my name.
I am standing too close to the leaf,
shallow-breathed as though I might
come into the eyes of this creature.

Sun burning down. I am a shadow
over teams of slow aphids. Everywhere
is green and light, shade and hunger.

The rush of a breeze pushes the wings—
the wasp could lift and drift to another
leaf, another green pile of clumsy food,
but desire dissipates as the air stills.

I do not want to leave that eloquent body
for this lumbering giant's. What purpose
would a breeze have for me?

I watch as it hovers a moment
before rising to float away.

Here, the Lily

Here, the lily, the broad hands
extend forward and open, inviting
your shadow to join its own:

wanting all of you—your darkness.
Did I say my hands, open in
invitation to the bright petal of you,

and the shadow you lay over me?
Yes, I raise my many hands in joy
like the good songs of the soil.

I take the rays of you, the light,
I grow because of that, I know, I
know and still I take the night

of you too, your shade and cool
balance. How could I not love
this contrast, this twilight,

when I am both the green shades
and bright whites and yellows—
rising up out of this rich soil?

Believing in Fire

Tonight, the trees are dreaming of fire.
They move their branches—
a primitive dance.
One reaches to another,
the vision is passed.
They whisper and hiss out
speaking in flame tongues.
Theirs is a hot prayer,
deliverance from the lumbering
destiny of becoming boards,
furniture, beaten and thinned to paper.

Their golden fantasy flickers
into religion. Belief in an afterlife
of seeds and extended spring.
Heaven has no chain saw, no mill.

Tonight, the trees dream of lightning,
the Creator's fast hand
sweeping over, sparking them
to rise in the starry firmament.

The Dandelion as the Wise One on the Mountain

There was no yellow
murmuring along the long
line of asphalt; no white velvet,
no applause of petals
for the wind, no black bee, no
water to drink, but I survived

in a high light, a burning noon,
open without shade. There were
others: bells, mandalas; always
a stem, a leaf, a green glimpse
and something, new, rising,
sprouting into the world;

saying, *Hello, hello!*
No matter how cruel the air,
I waited for a hush, or an exhale
from some creature crawling under,
scurried in rumors of stones—slow
herds that weighted the earth

kept the soil from dusting
away with each summer gust.
Dry dirt desirous
of waters that slumbered
in a far off lake-aloof,
calm as a coat of algae.

And what would I tell
a seeker should any come?
It was a bitter drought.
I am the witness, this is
my fact: I am here,
still afraid of fire and flood.

4. Aftermaths

You and Not You Drawing a Bath
—after a Paul Schulenburg painting

It is not as though she resembles you—
red hair pulled back and spilling down
the curve of her backbone. A darker
complexion, she is not like your frame—
she is thicker. Her robe slips to rest off her
shoulders in a way yours has never.
She leans forward (not like you've bent)
to turn the faucet, to draw a bath that you
would not take—certainly not in a late hour
of morning. Her face suggests this
will be a leisurely soak, lost time.
This is not you and yet there is no one
else I paint into the composition, outlined
by white window shutters that collect
the quiet of winter snow. Even though
I have not seen you in such blue light.

PAPER SOUL

folded into origami, to hide a burn hole
by a child's magnifying glass. A crane,
that does not look so much a bird,
but will fly with the first wind—as someone
says the word *littering*, and gives
a disapproving look with disgust. What water
does is make the white stiffness pliable
in its currents. The doodle, the phone number
for an interested stranger dissipates, leaving
a bright island for a desperate beetle—
the secret desire of salmon muscling the river.
A wordless ghost spinning out to an ocean.
The tide unfolds a wing first before it breaks
the body down into food for smaller mouths.

THE LOST LYRE

It was over the cobblestones of a plaza,
close to winter's edge, that a filtered light
brightened the brick facades. He heard
angels singing. He bent his ear
but could not tell from where the voices
arose. For years he sought their music.
Through the avenues of New York, Sydney,
Beijing, Cape Town and other cities,
following hums, faint notes drifting
around corners. In Verona, clouds of voices
billowed around him, moved him through
ambered streets, the knotted alleyways,
the music intensifying with each step
till his fingers twitched like plucked strings,
and his skin rippled with each overwhelming
tone. And there in the shadowed heart
of the city he stopped and turned back,
having found the lost music, the source—
the scarred and nicked lyre within his body.

The Hidden Cells

My best love poem is hidden
in the cells of a spreadsheet,
tucked away between annual
corporate revenues. This is what
I feel is lacking from the ledger
sheets, the final balance:
lines written with passion

about the starlight reflected
off her hair. How she and I are
the perfect merger—
my belly fitting into the curve
of her spine, the mix of our salt.
Sweet salt, how once empires
were lost or conquered,

treasuries built from it.
In one cell of this spreadsheet
is more wealth than all
the pharaohs stole.
A salt sky to hold
my metaphors, my symbols
of the mathematics

between the two of us.
Here I keep record of trade,
cash and equivalents, income
taxes, the cost of production,
the price of an average share,
current assets, inventories,
and the gross profits of love.

Sirens

Orpheus knew the music before his shipmates
heard the spindrift tones, high notes over
the ocean's horizon. Seductive in their simplicity,
good licks, but merely a trick, almost amateurish
in nature. He had the mastery to destroy, to pluck
the singers from the sky with a sound, a bright tune
that would shear their wings, send them spiraling
into the sea, a shark's meal for sure. He was still
in awe of an orderly universe and knew the song
birds served a purpose like whales and porpoises.
So he set his strings to wail an inspired verse, nearly
prophetic, about young men living a life of questing
and lovers so strong as to disrupt the realm of gods.

MEDUSA IN SMALLVILLE

She forgot herself and ran bare-footed out to the street
yelling at her new ex's rusted, pick-up speeding away,
taillight broken. She is braless in her around-the-house t-shirt
and old panties. Her fist raised toward the yellowed
moon her hair dark snakes tonguing the wild stars.
The smell of burnt tires mingles with the hay and cow
manure, wafts around her feet aching from the asphalt.
Now she can see the familiar black triangles from parted
curtains, she dreams the myriad whispers —*look
she's at it, again*— and sees herself completely
middle-aged, a gorgon, drunk and out of cigarettes
and liquor, and no one to drive her down to the all-night store.
She is a statue in the street caught in a reflection.
She remembers being the prom queen, a social butterfly
with fingers pulling the strings of every man. How did she
forget herself? And where did that girl go?

Circe Waiting

Standing in the low light of embers,
as the scythe-like moon pierces another cloud,
she watches the horizon, tries to remember
the shape of your ship, the words you had vowed.
She twitches a finger and an animal yelps
but all of the joy that she once would have felt
is flat as her bedsheets and nothing will help.
With a spell from her lips every anchor melts.
She's stripped down to skin and resolved to stare
at the fish-glistening sea with her cat eyes.
While plucking thin bones of pig and of hare
she puts out a tune that sends all ships awry.
She tortures the sailors, snaps their limbs like oars,
tearing into their bodies as though it were yours.

Dreaming Poetry of Hydrogen

My dreams burn like Hindenburg
zeppelins in the gray morning.
I rub hot ashes in my eyes,
straining to cry for the loss of fantasy.
I could be a painted witch-doctor,
but minute hands of rain would wash
away the facade.
Does this mask look good?
I cannot tell.
It was built from inside to out.
Hydrogen is burning quicker,
only the flaming skeleton remains
to come crashing down.

In a room full of Gods,
none shall fear my bones.

WOMAN AND WINDOW LIGHT
—after a painting by Paul Schulenburg

Sunlight ghosting through the glass—
the furniture cuts right through it.
Juncos on the other side

of a windowed life, back-lit, dark
against the cement, are greedy

bickering over the seeds I gave out
moments ago. This is all the same

as it was yesterday—even this
thought. The aspens are turning

into an imitation of fire, again.

I am waiting for the ravens to return,
to bully the small birds away

and gather their black chasm eyes,
a cancer coming back from remission

restoring the lengthening night.

Casida of a Rising Woman
    —*After Federico Garcia Lorca*

I think you are obsessed with nakedness—
always on about smooth hills and rounded ponies.
You speak as though the earth is revealing itself,
giving you its secret, another reason to live.

I never wanted to be naked, never wanted
rainwater to roll from my shoulders,
to trickle and pool, a place of light,
a place of your reflection.

Do not speak of blood—no, I will not hear it tonight,
with our brothers' war so close outside the door—
keep the words in your heart, that dark closet
where your let your true violet blossom.

Don't touch my belly with your wanting fingers
swimming in the coral dawn light on my horizon.
Keep your talk of roses blooming. Ignore the dead,
their boots, the artillery pounding our town.

The Cannonball

You might see it there: the blue-
black night edging against her flying.
How the golden web catches, breaks her

speed, the arc of descent.
If she were another sort of creature,
The primary-colors costume and sequins

would catch the fast jaws of a predator.
The white gloves on splayed hands
would twitch the hunger of a hunter.

With a boom she breaks
through the huge paper star
and the aria of the audience's *ahh!*

She's learned the art of physics:
mass and velocity, gymnastics.
To hold for a moment of weightlessness

before the fetal-curl falling. She is used
to the afterscent of gunpowder
in her hair, accustomed to air

coursing round her body. She dreams
of flying without her leather skin. Now
she feels gravity as a punishment

for some unconfessed sin.
Was it the tightrope walker,
the acrobat or the barker

who gasped watching her fall
back to the patient earth?
Not all the stars are made of paper,

and that is where her heart stays—
aloof to projectiles that puncture the stars
for a crowd of approval.

She presents a prayer to the Flying Saints
and lowers into the mouth of the cannon.
She is born with her mass under velocity,

A soaring cross, outstretched
for redemption and she feels Newton's ghost
crawl the length of her spine.

She is close to being air, her body
makes exchanges with other molecules.
Here, she thinks of arms flattening to wings,

But whistled heaviness fills her, pulls her
into a red ball, bright bullet speeding back.
She groans out again,

*Lord, whose name is an engine's roar, reshape
me an angel, a messenger, your harbinger
of doom, in return for true flight.*

More Than Sound

the voice is sometimes the shadow
of the body lost on a sidewalk
beneath the rumbling city.

The voice is not always present
during rainstorms or making brief
appearances like lightning flashes.

In the dimness of a solitary room
the voice fills the body of the listener
or the lover,

and in this hollowness,
long before the light enters,
the shadow has become comfortable.

ULYSSES TAKES THE A-TRAIN TO CALYPSO'S APARTMENT

He is drawn to the building like it has gravity—
to pick her lock, to sit on her balcony
and search over the busy lights of the city.

She gave him the answers he lacked in his life:
how to clean-up; stop being a big phony;
and find a way back to his house and his wife.

He returns again, hoping he'll get another epiphany.

PERSEPHONE AT THE FARMERS' MARKET

Even now, I cannot lose the memory of scent.
It leads me to pomegranates, halved, lying on a table,
the globes of puckered skin are red as my own lips.
This is the season of abduction—fruit pulled
from branches and vines. The dense perfumes
of fresh jams and pies slice the slow dawn.
The maples and oaks turn thin and gray
with their testimony of bruised and bloodied leaves.
Drawn to the sanguine, tart sugar, ripe aroma,
hundreds of lusting eyes, I touch the dark
texture and remember my love's rough hands,
the frantic tear and pull of desire.
I hand my money to the farm boy, grab
the pomegranate —*no, I don't need a bag*—
and rush away to dark home. Pulling it apart,
the ruby juice bleeding out on my fingers and dress,
I close my lips around the sweet flesh
and dream of the man my husband used to be.

Your Star Chart is Finite

You see the constellation of yourself
more clearly than the ghosts near you:
a man standing with hands posed on hips—
steady as a pilot, not one to sail unwisely
into a sleeve of fog. You've spent hours
connecting the stars, naming them: *Love,
Honor, Loyalty, Fortitude, Faith, Virtue,
Career, Family, Money*. But you have
begun to focus on the faint lights swimming
the black sea within your boundaries: *Greed,
Lust, Abandon, Wanton, Vice, Selfishness*.
Their combined gravity pulls at your face,
poison ingested. You feel dark, empty
as the space between suns, each sight
of yourself in the sky is a reminder
of imperfections, blind to the brighter
lights that mark your place in the night.

Against Against Metaphor

I still cannot carry my broken sound
down to the grave of Metaphor, to nod and cry

as someone prattles on about *its time*.
In this deserted hour, I watch the bullfrog stars

hunger for crickets. Where is the pond
that used to be here, reflecting—an answer

to the lonely dome of the world? What drought
has descended on the heart of this field?

In this failing light, I cannot make out
where the marker stands, or what it says.

The words are small birds, finches and grosbeaks,
free flying in marble archways. They echo.

You see, I've done it again, my Beloved:
caged an image with expression.

Snow Globe Life

Always there were two kinds of weather:
days when the snow lay heavy
and three kids bobbed in their snow shoes,
dragging a sled to some hill
just beyond the fingerprint sky;

those other days of earthquakes
and blizzards, their smiles leaned
to grimaces, cheeks flushed as flurries.

Each of them prays to god
for a dusty dome of sky,
left alone to endless snowball fights,
a dog bouncing in the drifts,
the next great sled run,
the longest day of winter.

IDOL

Orpheus was gifted a godly lyre
and assumed he was The Best. Not once
did he think there could be someone better
out there, perhaps in a poorer neighborhood,
with an ear for robins and finches,
who knew the inner tones of the world
and could repeat them, a child who heard
the high pitches that set dogs whining
and the deep drum beats of the dead.
It never occurred to Orpheus he was not
the best — no, he just stroked the strings,
sung what came too easily, and always
believed the things his press agent said.

AFTER READING YOUR LETTERS

Flooding toward the river
with schools of moons,
I followed an odd light.
A poplar lent me its shadow.
I carried your pages
safely in my body.
Autumn turned us to red and yellow.
I responded with such hummingbirds,
I could not write a reply.

SONNET

The man would not sleep in his bed.
She had written on the stretched
white sheet a love sonnet in lipstick.

They would have made love on it
when she returned home,
but she never came back.

The man discovered the poem the next night.

He slept with the dog on the floor
at the foot of the bed,
both curled and crying.

After her funeral he couldn't sleep.
Months fell away from his mind.

The dog worried behind him
from room to room.
The phone never rang.

One night when he'd forgotten her touch,
he went through photographs
to remember her smile.
He cleaned and scrubbed the grieving house
like they used to do together.
He showered and shaved,
lit a candle in the bedroom,
lay naked on the bed.

He slept with her verse.
The red words were printed on his body.
The next morning he stood at the mirror
reading new messages from the dead.

BIRTHDAY NOTE

A savant provides the exact number of minutes to a life.
It is November and the Dryads are clinging to their leaves.

I feel myself thinner than before.
Beneath the darkening sky my own light is warmer.

My habits are shed the way a cocoon of an overcoat
is removed to reveal flannel wings.

Further disrobing. I emerge from the layers,
as someone I nearly knew. A new version of my old self

standing at the anniversary party; bare, in a room
full of meteorologists — unafraid of the weather.

Acknowledgments:

Poems in this book have appeared in the following magazines: *Alba; Animus; Chariton Review; Clackamas Literary Review; Clay Palm Review; Controlled Burn; Eclipse; Ellipsis; The Elemental Chart of Poetry; Gargoyle; Gravity; Hotel Amerika; In Posse; Interim; Lilies and Cannonballs Review; Mississippi Review; Mochila Review; The National Poetry Review; North American Review; Pacific Review; Pilgrimage; Poetry East; Porcupine; Portland Review; Potpourri; Puerto Del Sol; The Rockhurst Review; Runes; Santa Clara Review; Shenandoah; Silhouettes Against the Electric Sky; Slipstream; Snow Monkey; White Noise* [UK]

"Auricle" was chosen as a runner up in the 2005 MR Prize and was published by the *Mississippi Review* as such.

"Auricle" was reprinted in *Good Times Weekly*, December 13th, 2006.

"Jesus in America", "Without End", "Medusa in Smallville" and "After Reading Your Letters" appeared in the chapbook, *What Language* (Slipstream, 2002).

"Persephone at the Farmer's Market" and "Departing Phoenix" were reprinted on *Verse Daily*.

The author gives his utmost gratitude to C. J. Sage for her editorial suggestions regarding this book and the author also wishes to thank the following people (in alphabetical order) for their suggestions regarding poems within this book: David Bolduc; Ilya Kaminsky; Kathleen Lynch; Andrew Roberts; and Hannah Stein.